Fruit Coloring Book Young Kids Learners A–Z

Author:
Sikandar Sami

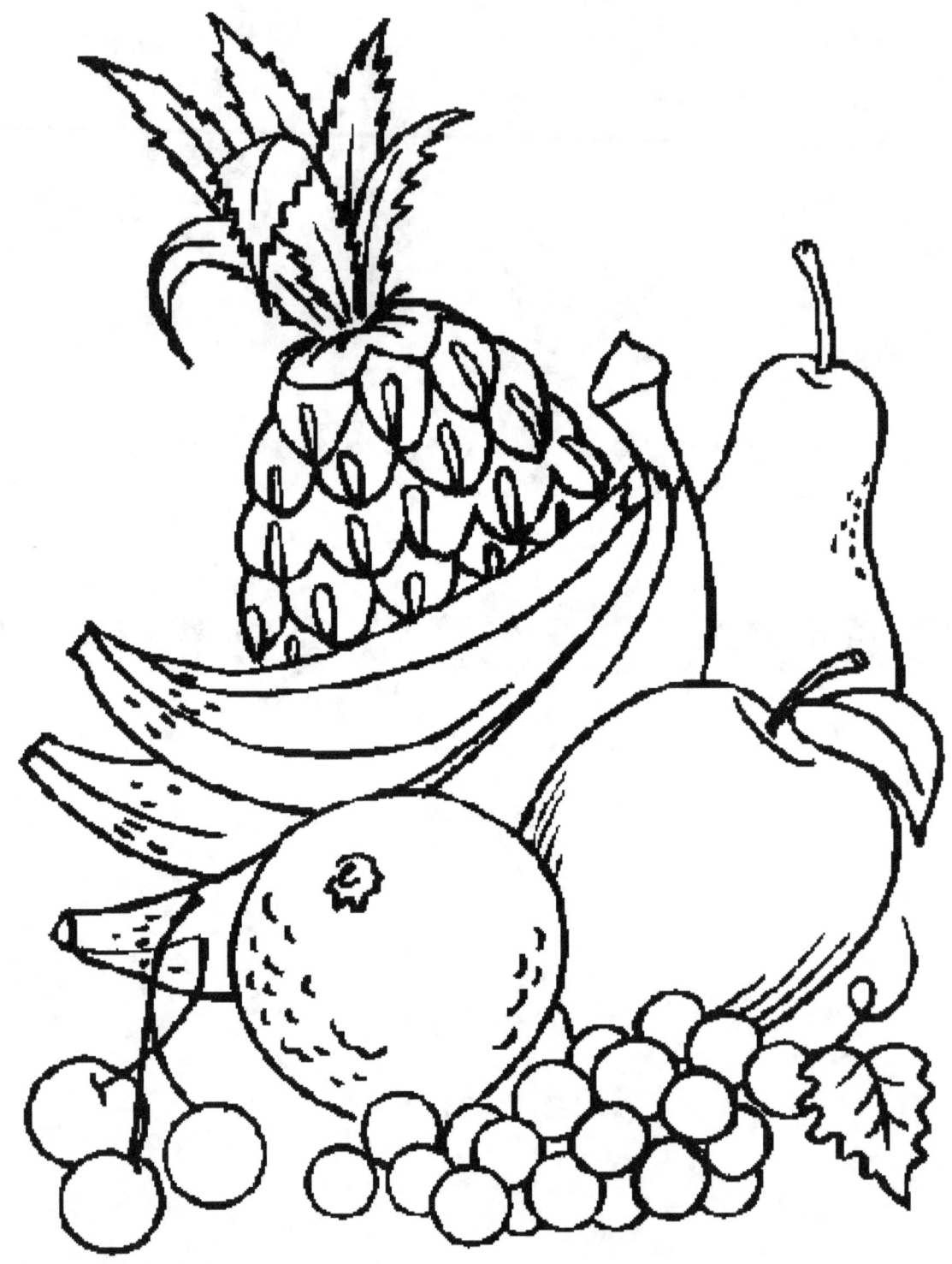

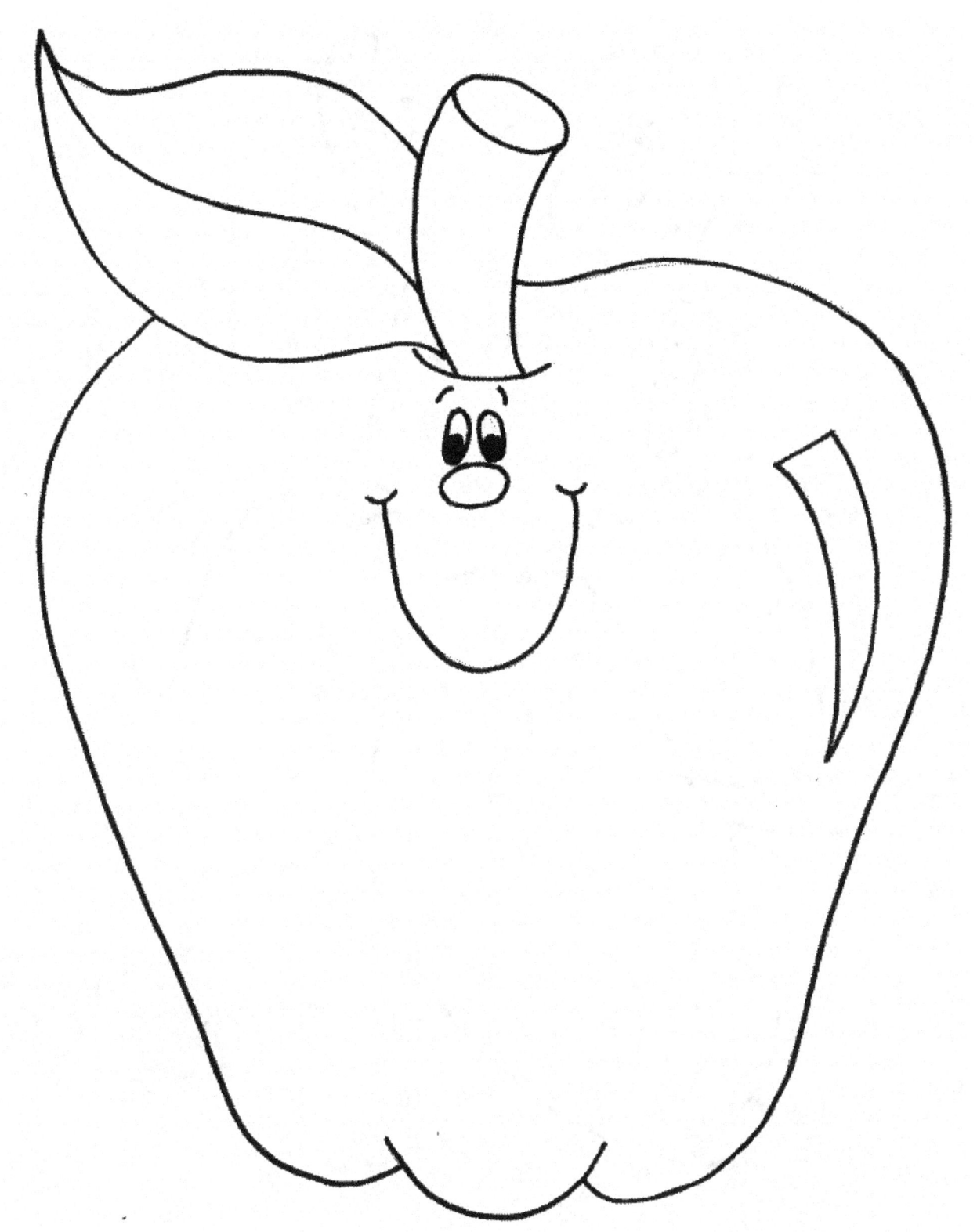

A is for Apple

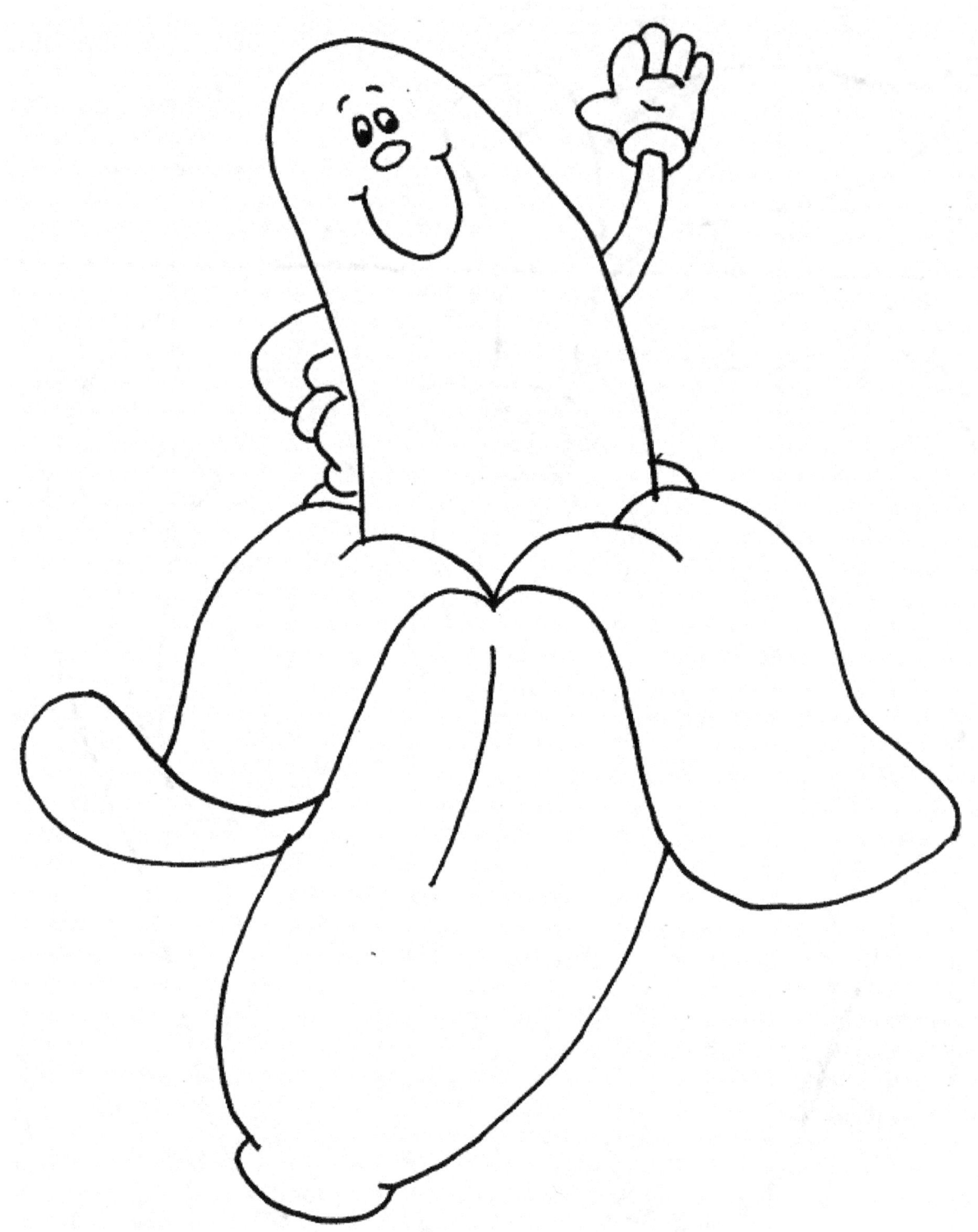

B is for Banana

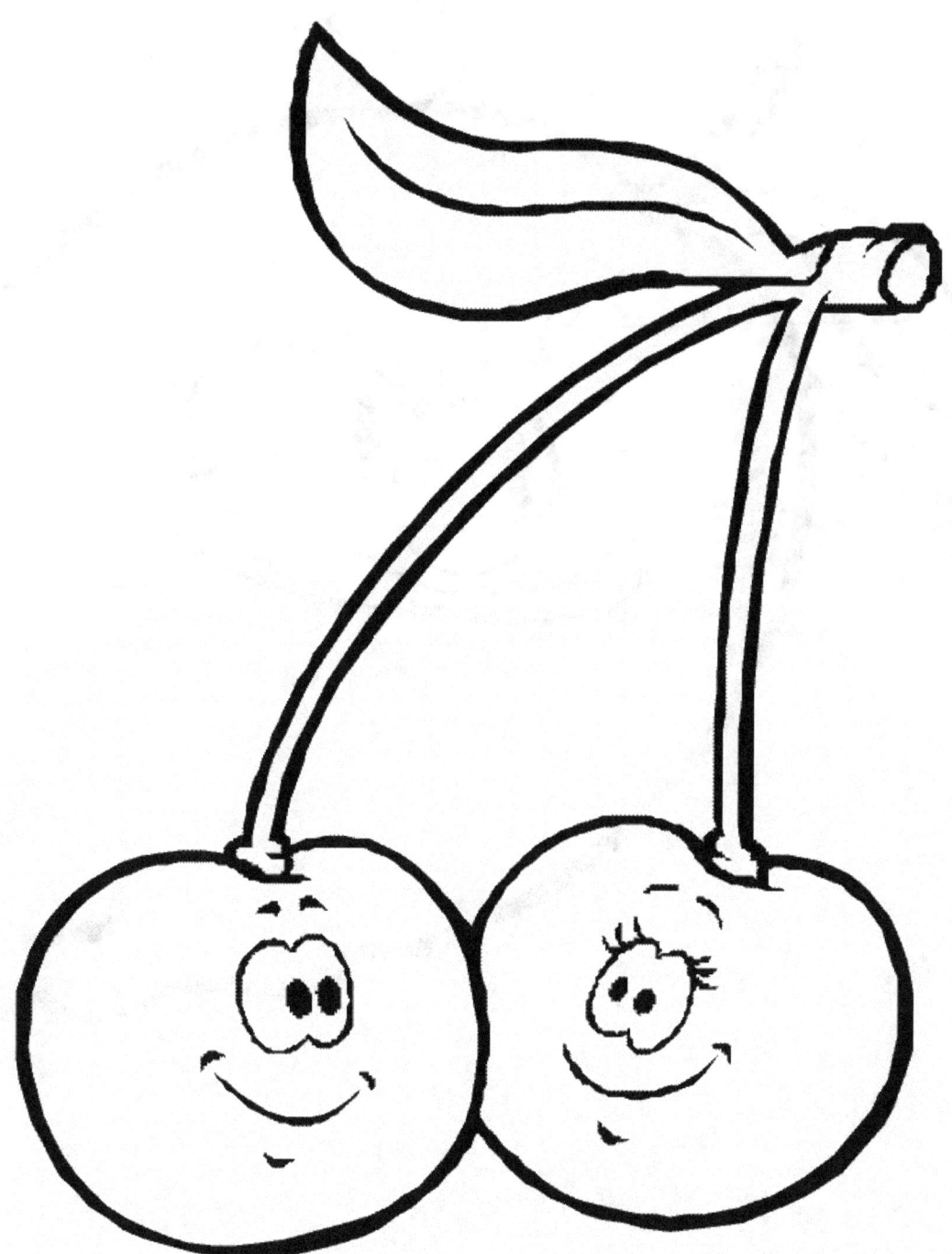

C is for Cherry

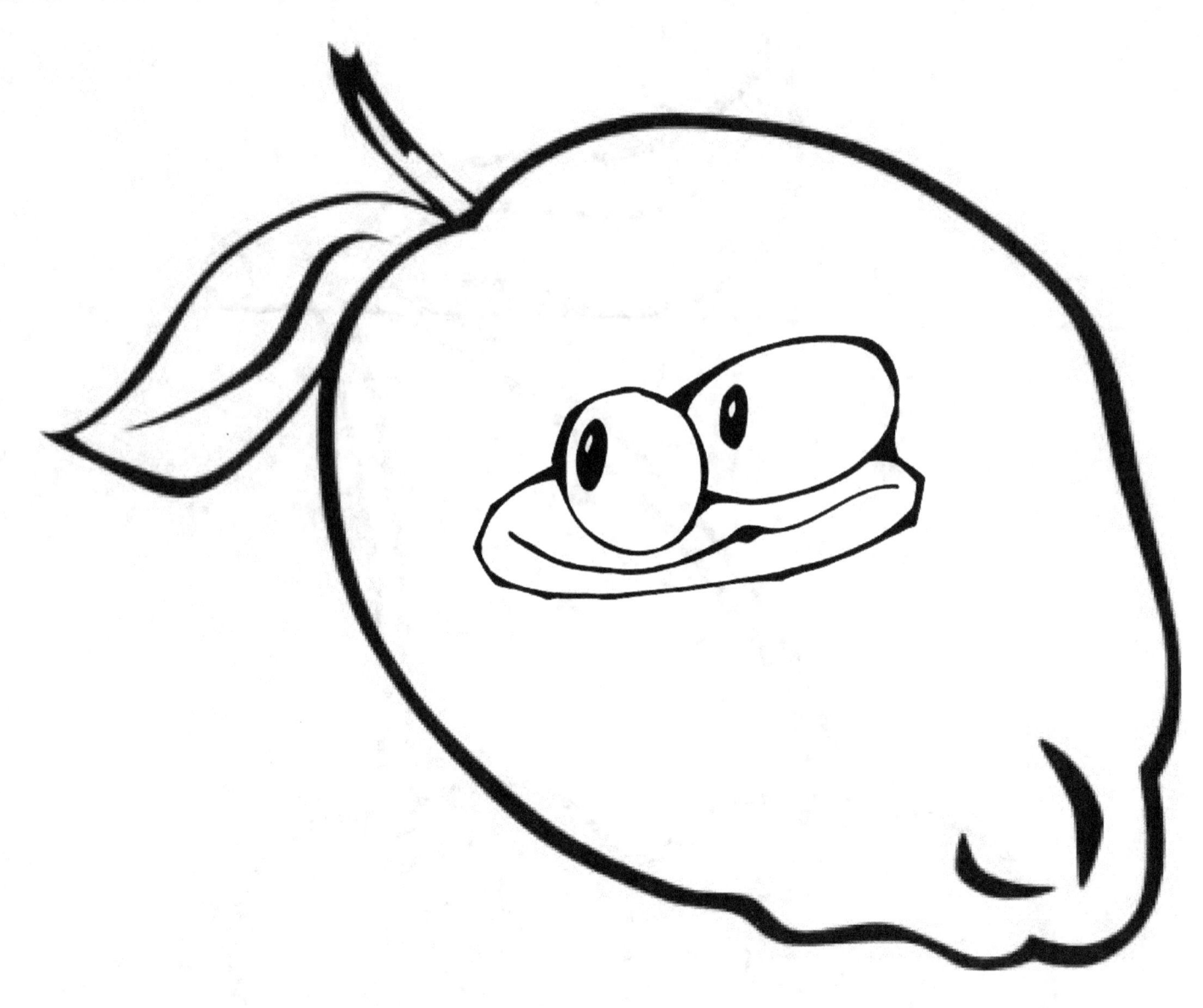

D is for a Date Fruit

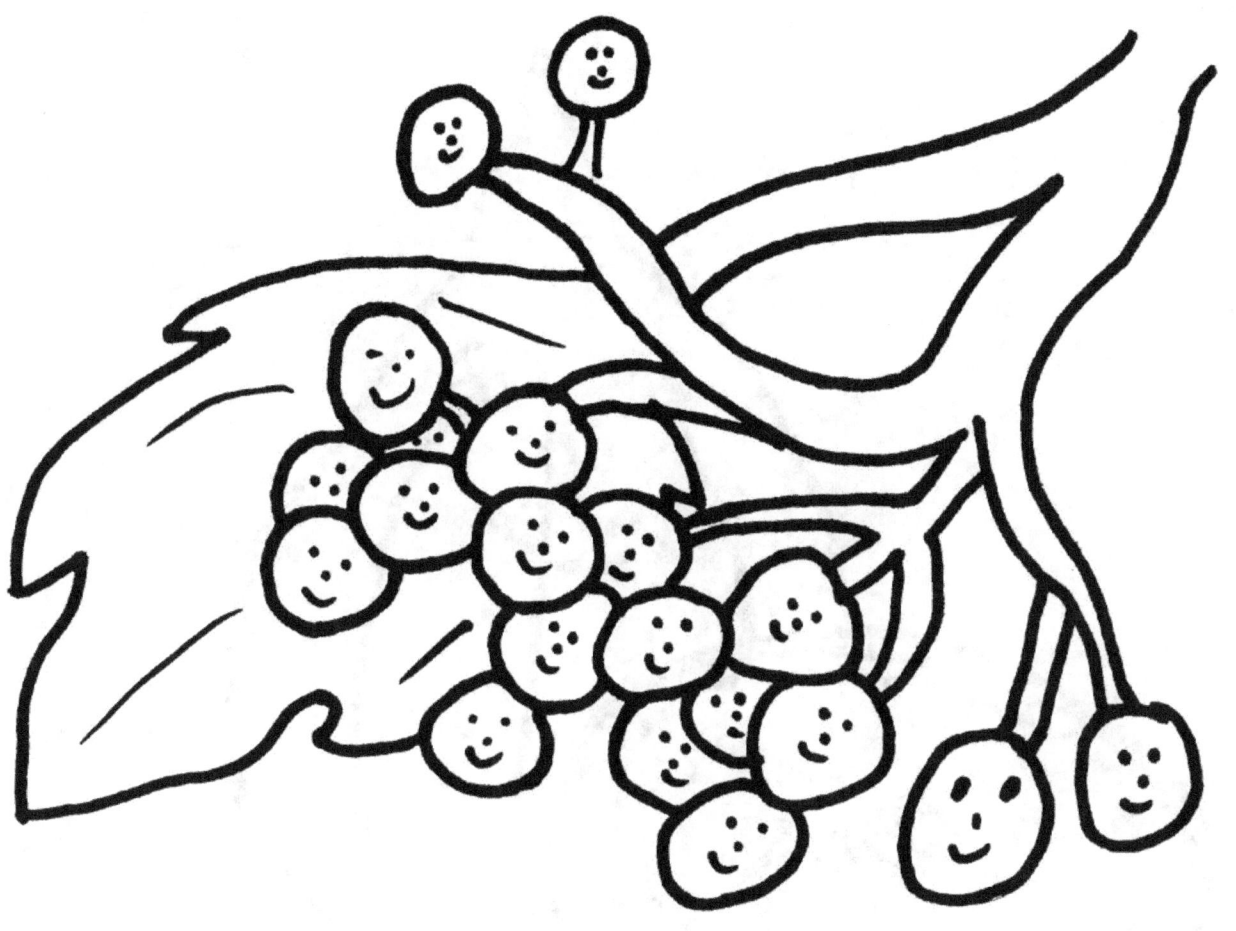

E is for Elderberries

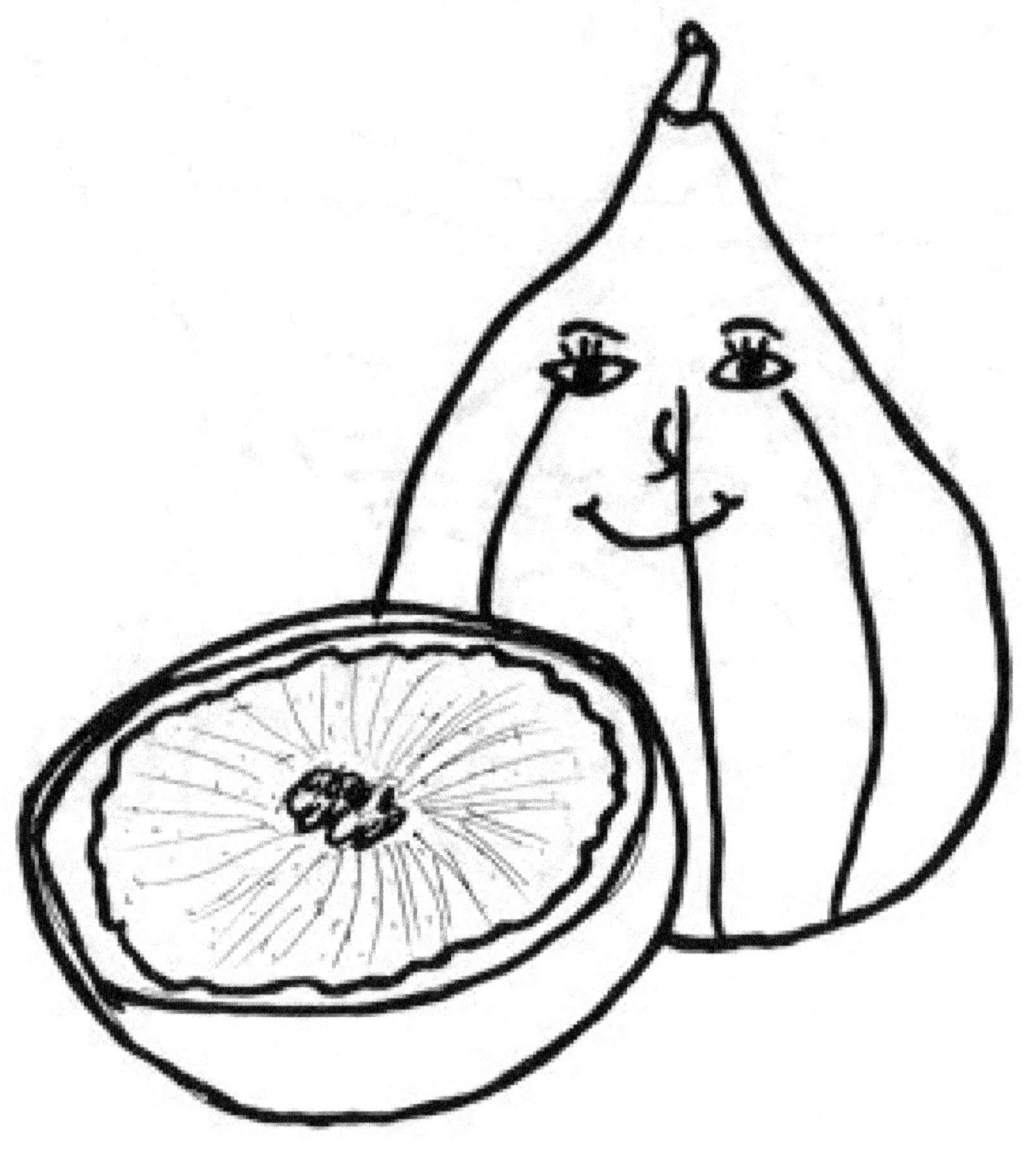

F is for Fig

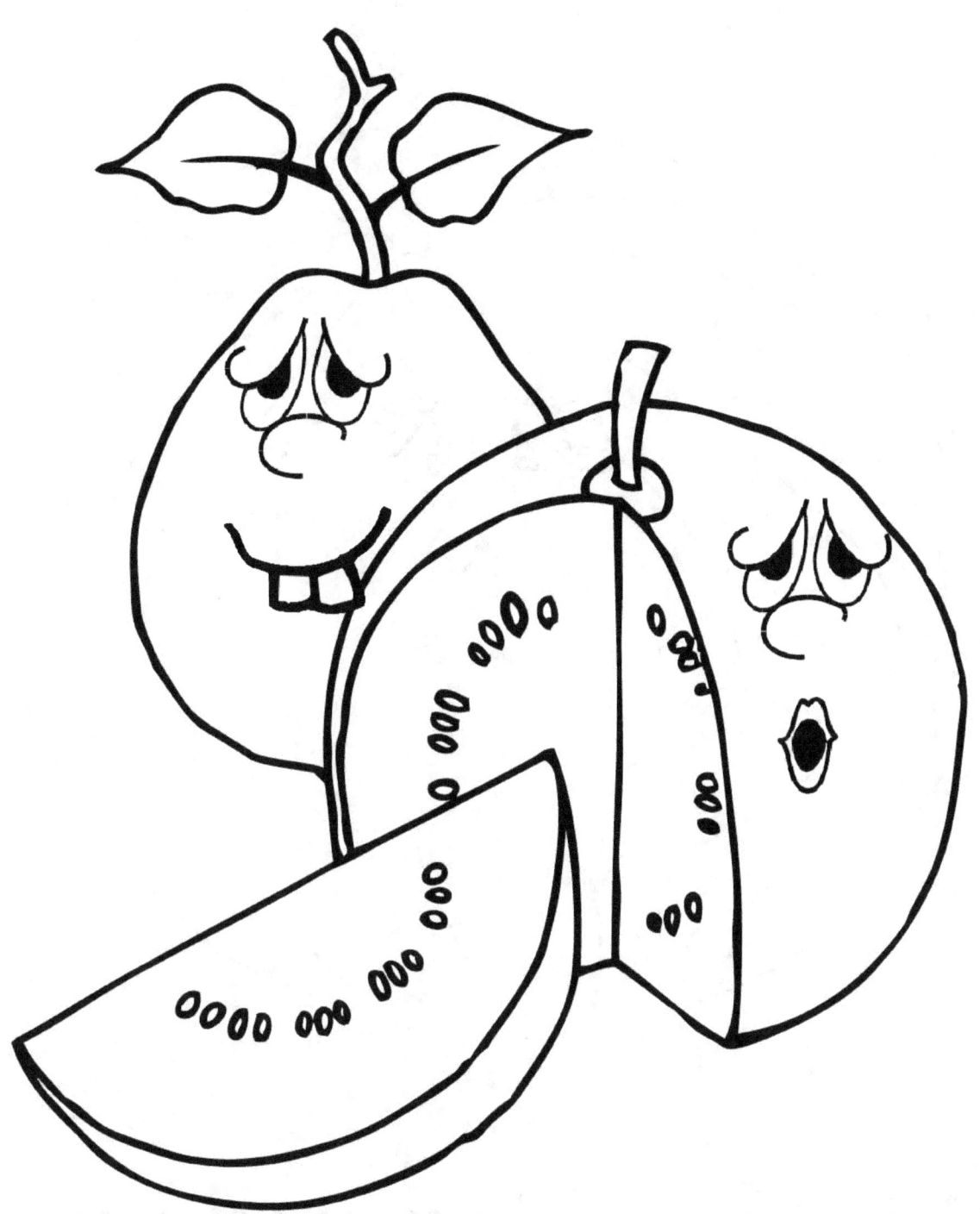

G is for Guava

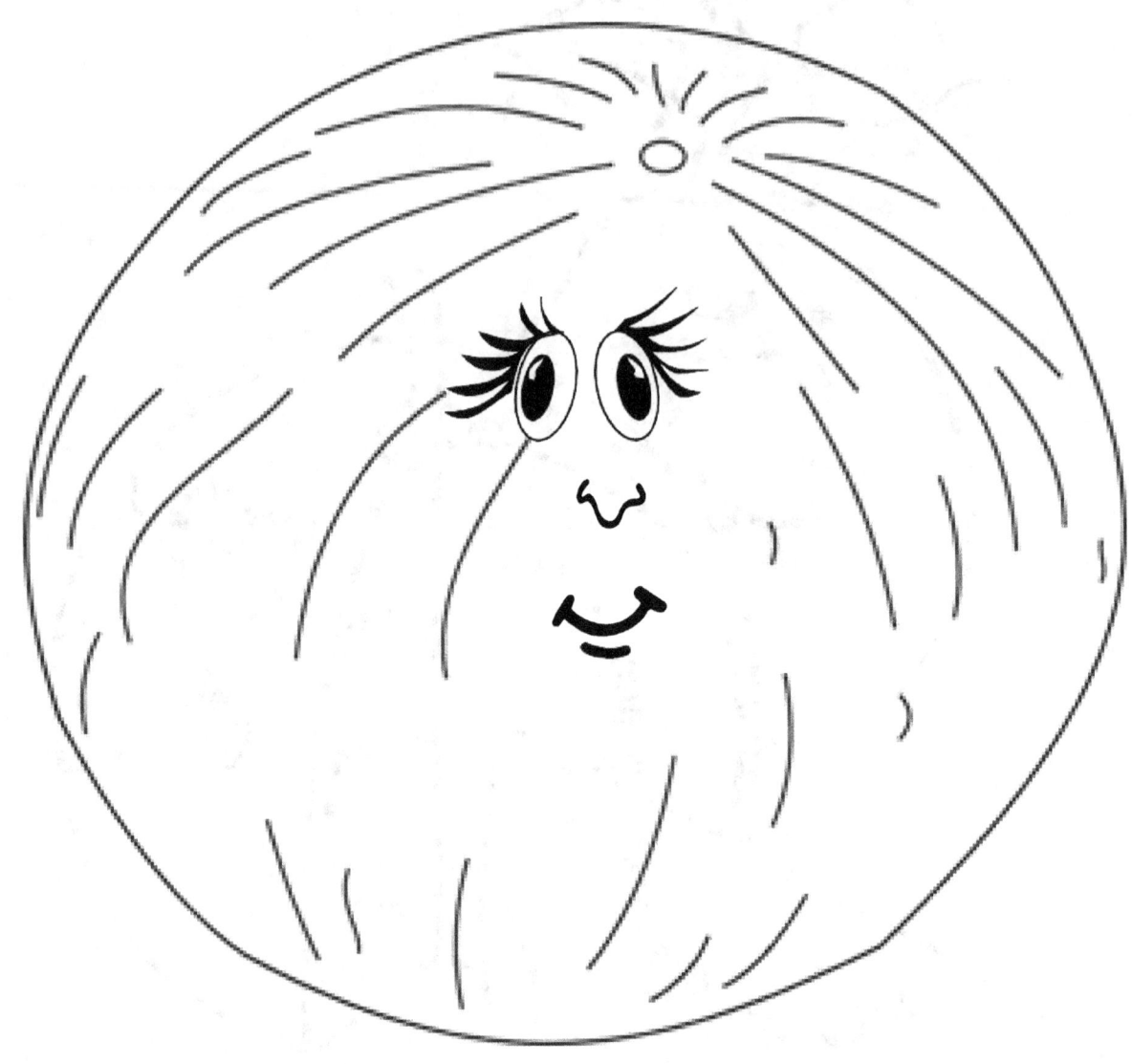

H is for Honeydew

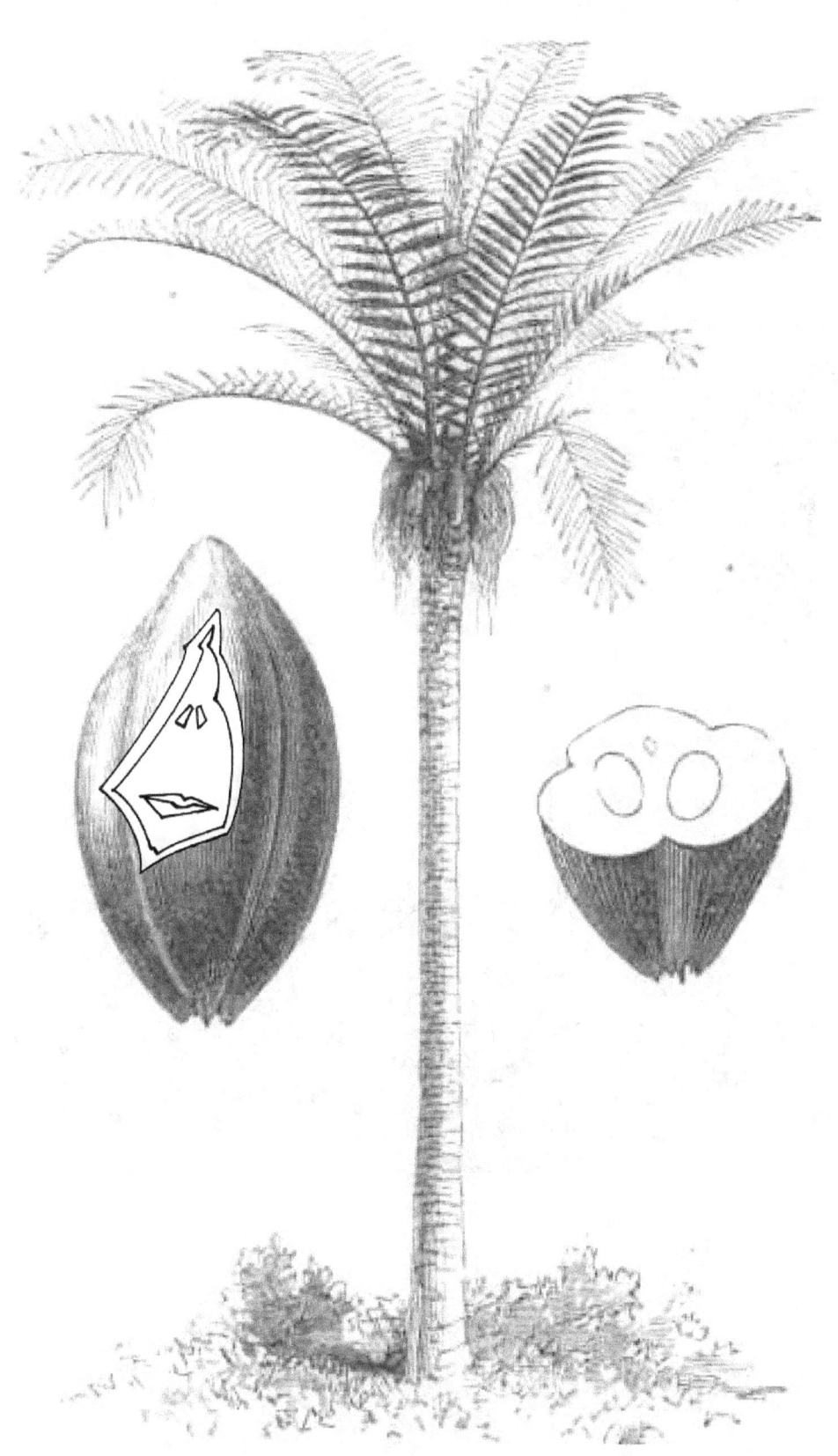

I is for Ita Palm Fruit

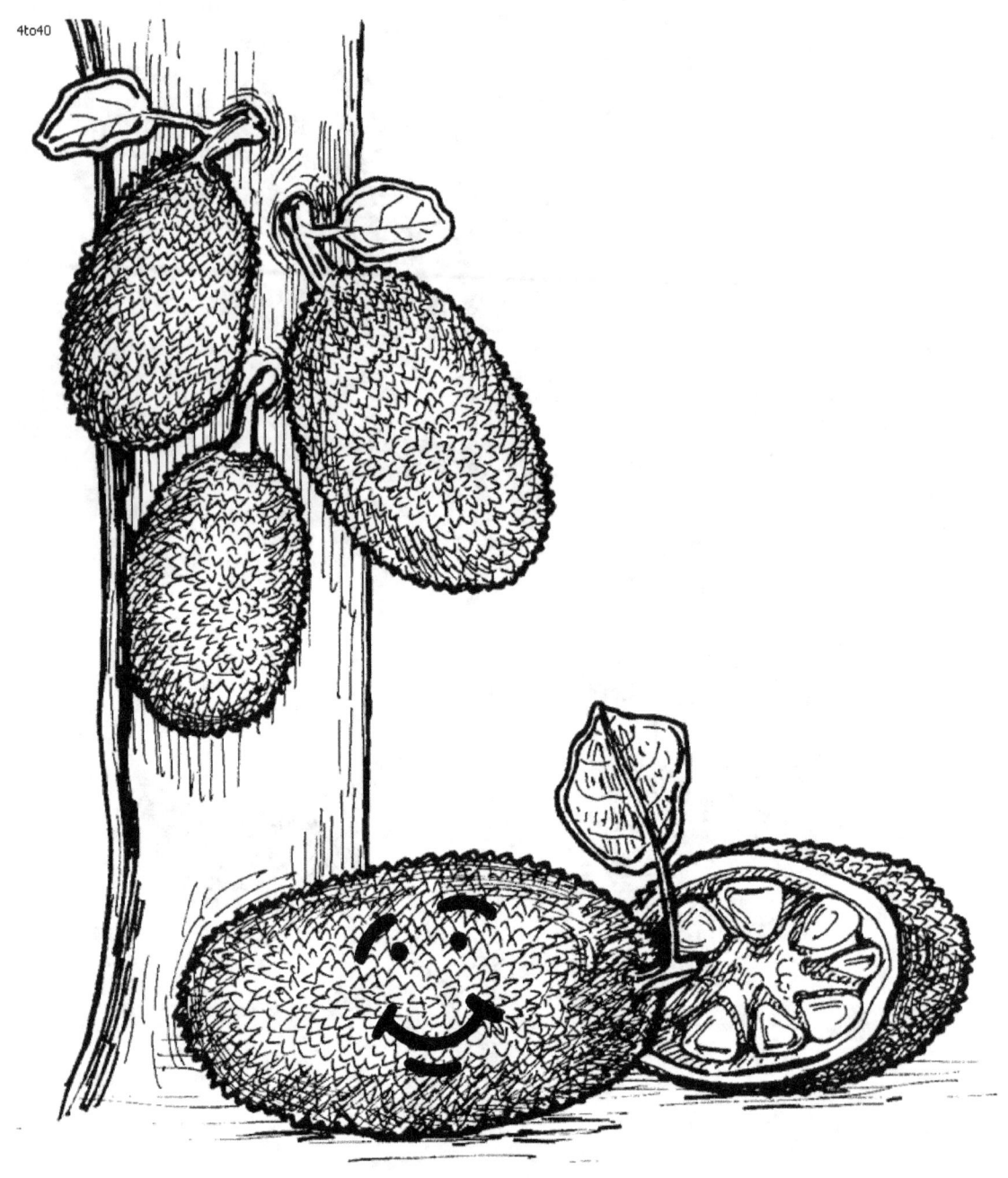

J is for Jackfruit

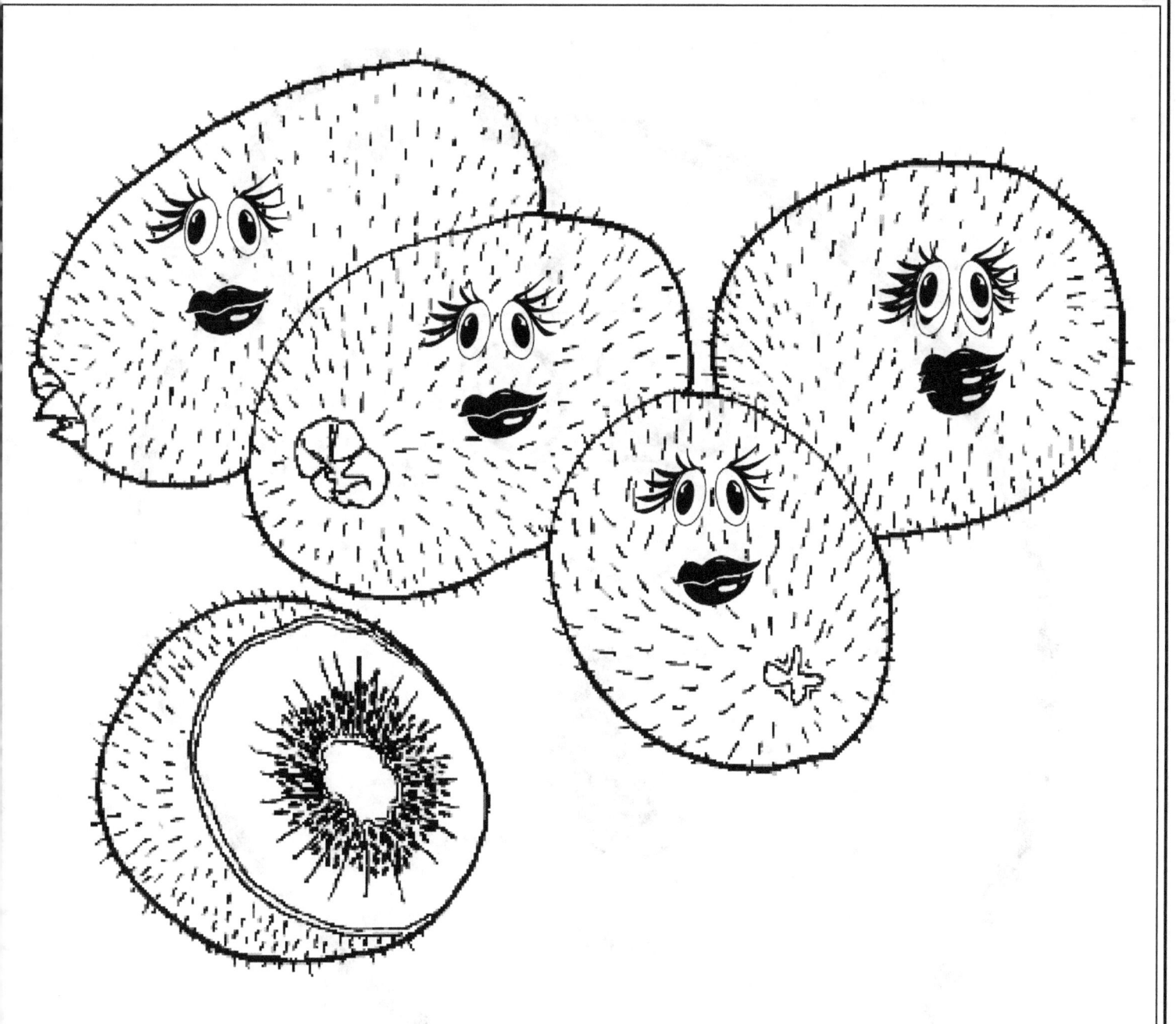

K is for Kiwi

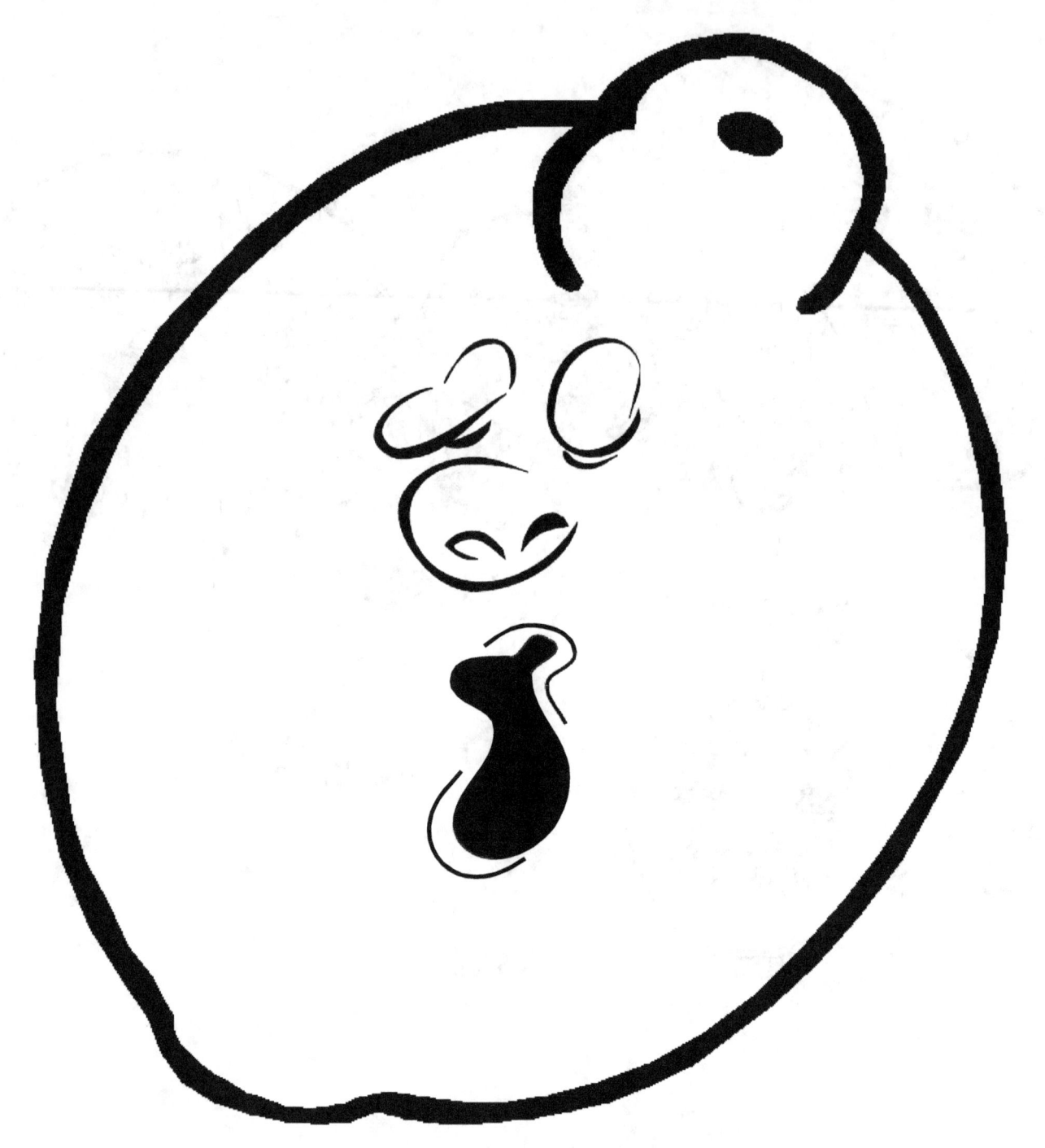

L is for Lemon

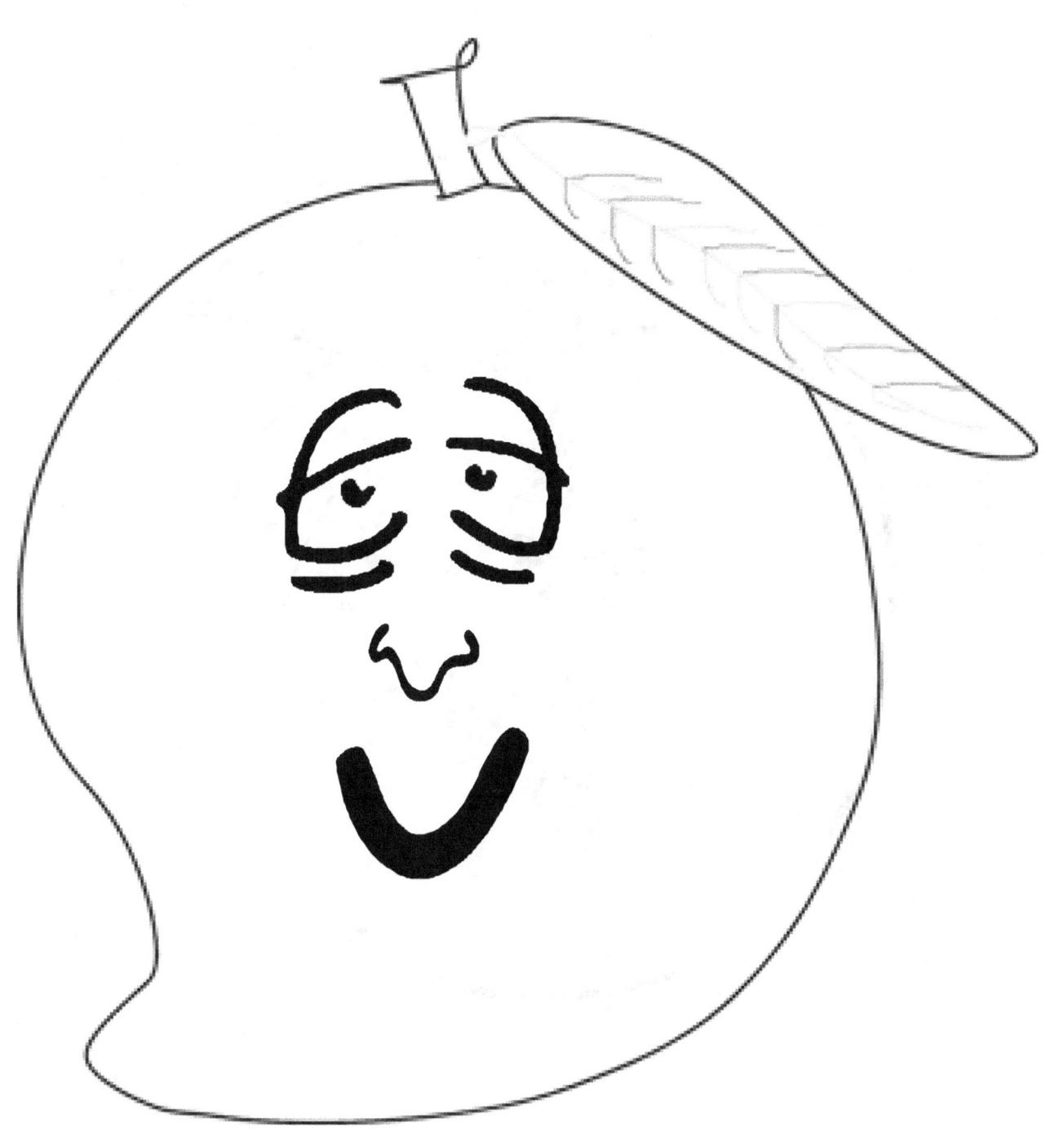

M is for Mango

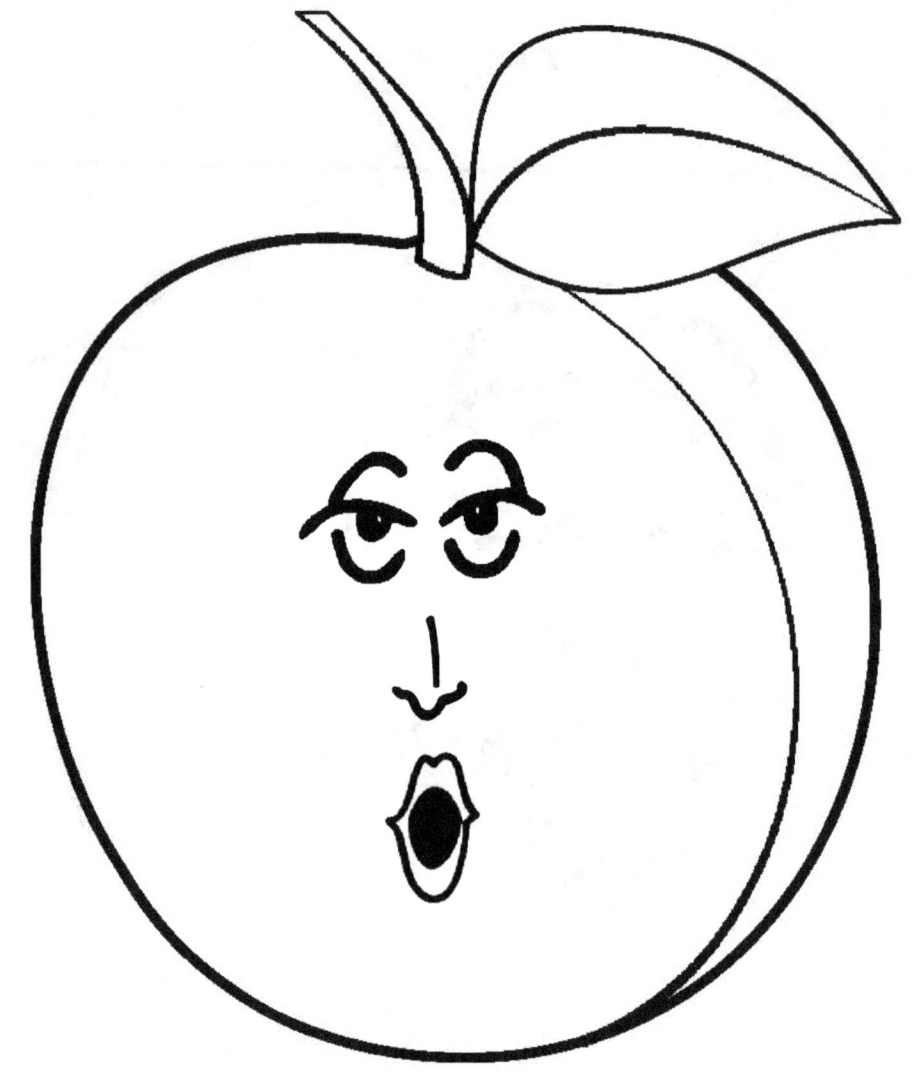

N is for Nectarine

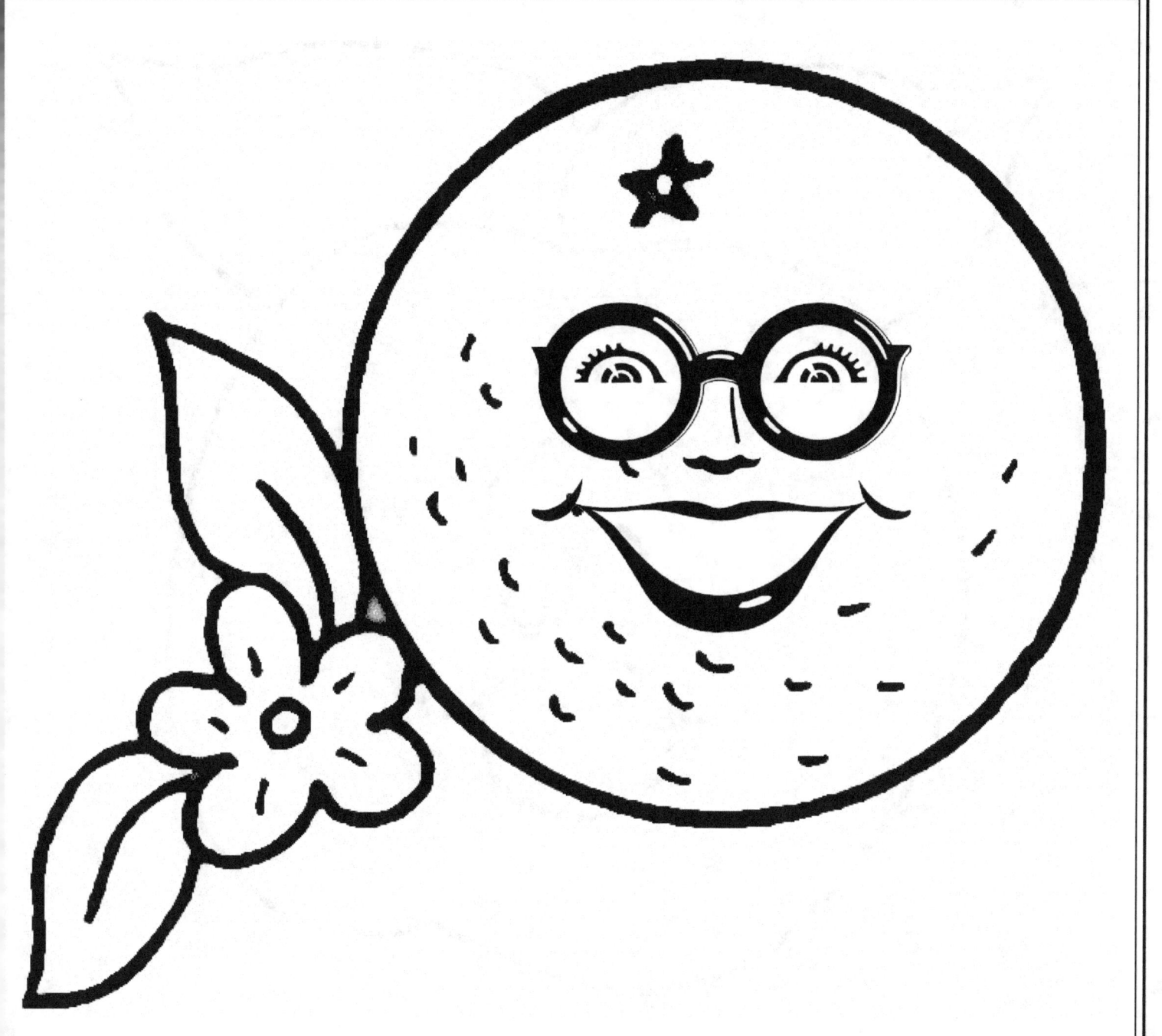

O is for Orange

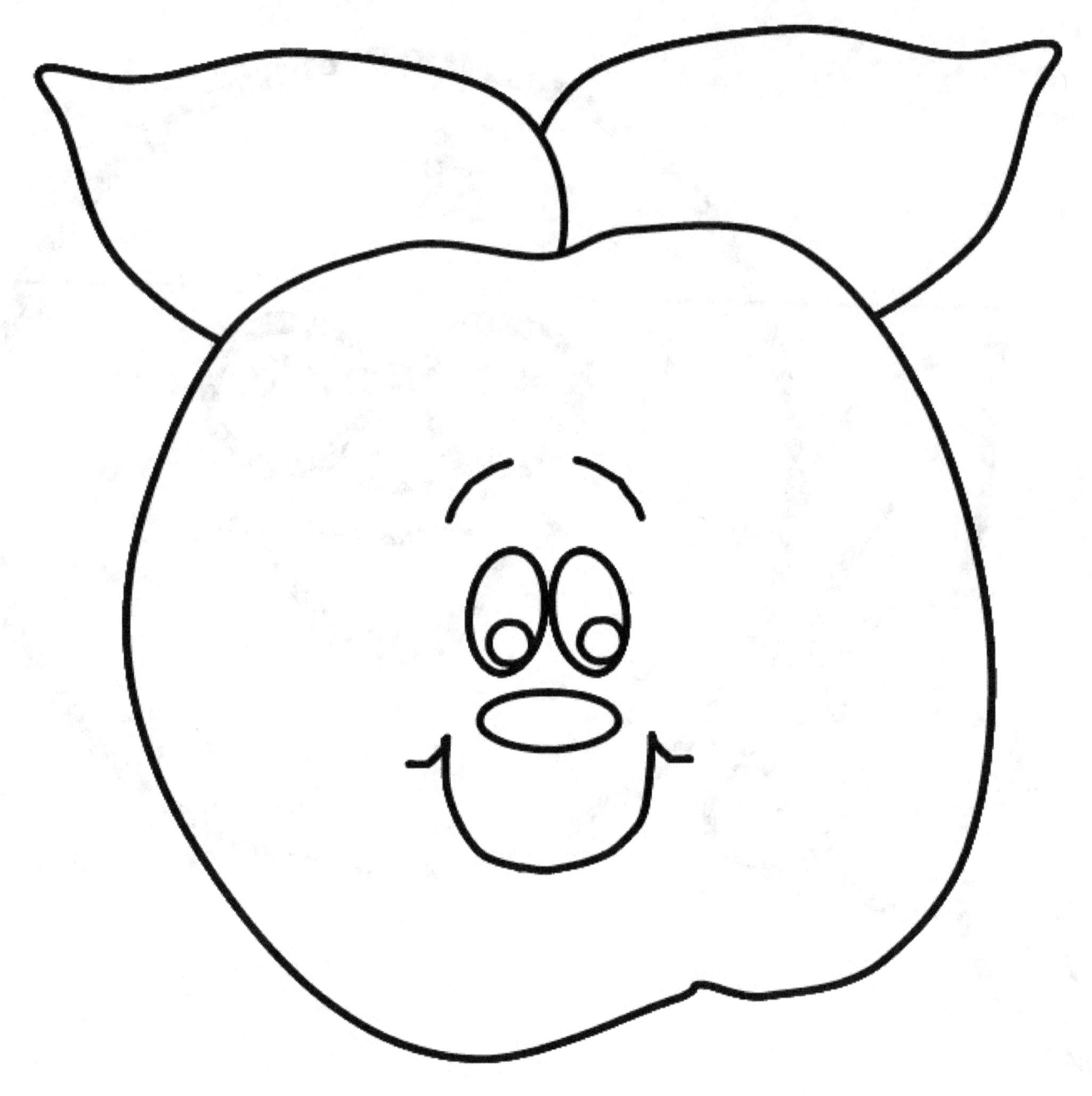

P is for Peach

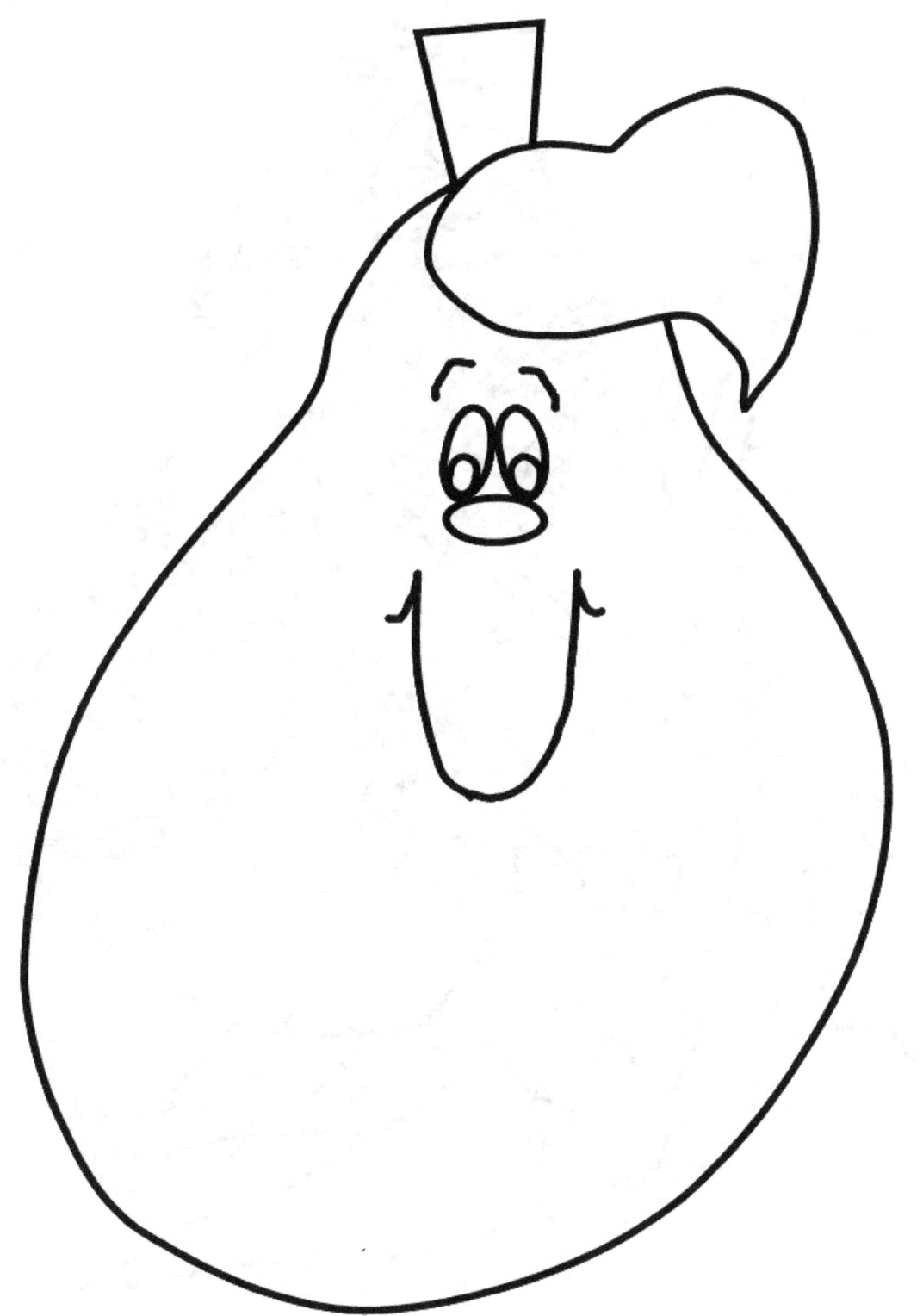

Q is for Quince Pear

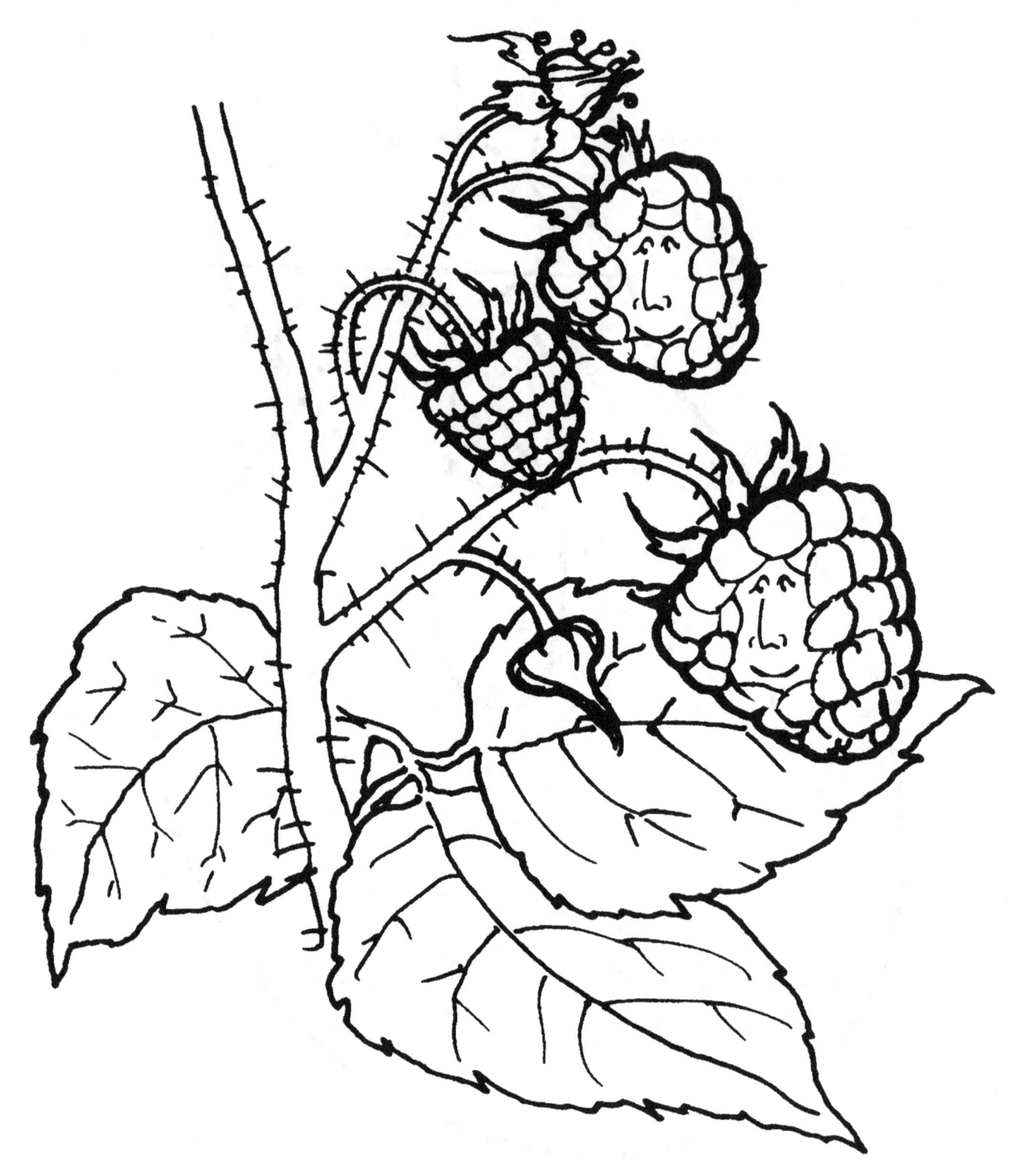

R ᎡᎠᏍᏆ Raspberry

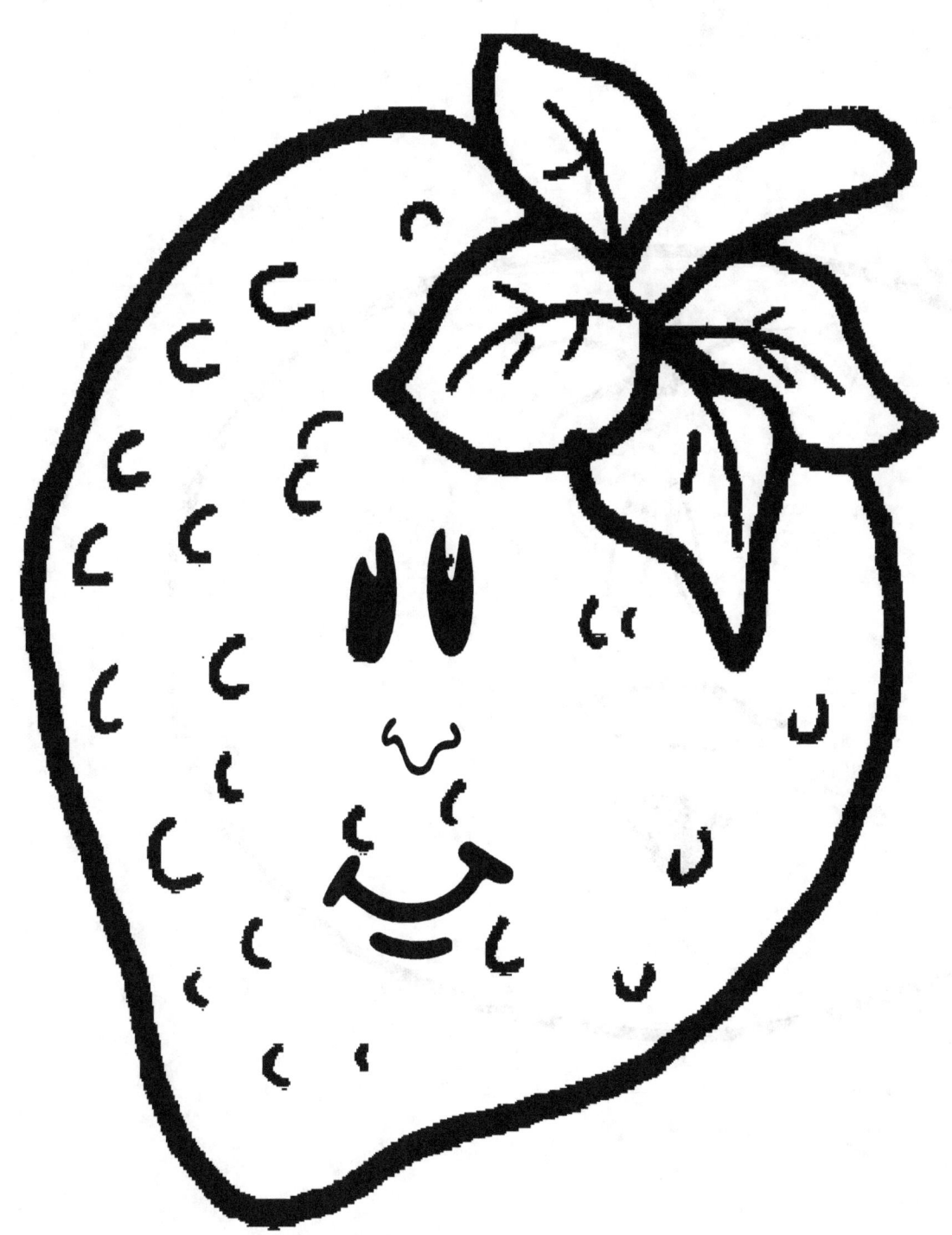

S is for Strawberry

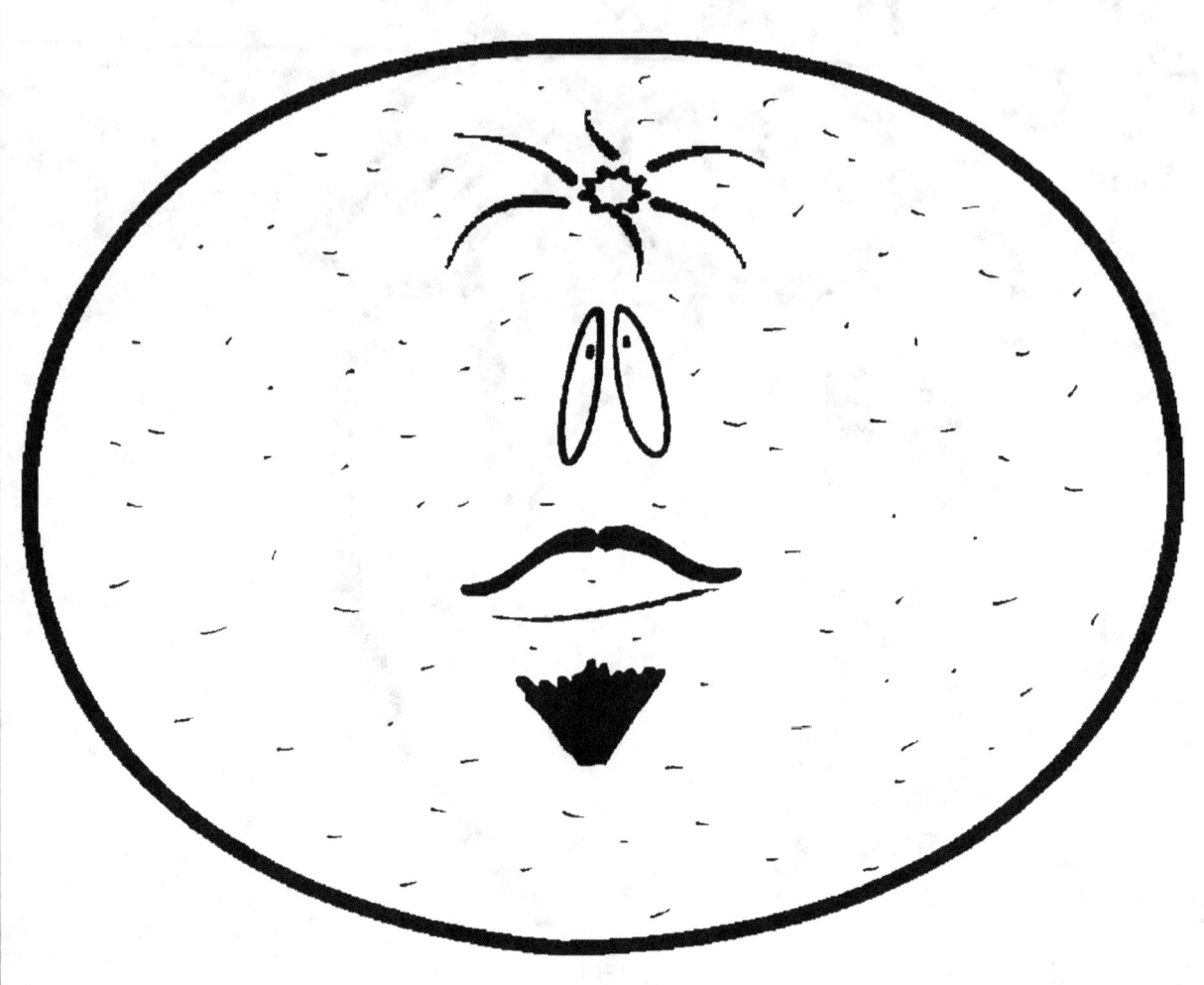

T is for Tangerine

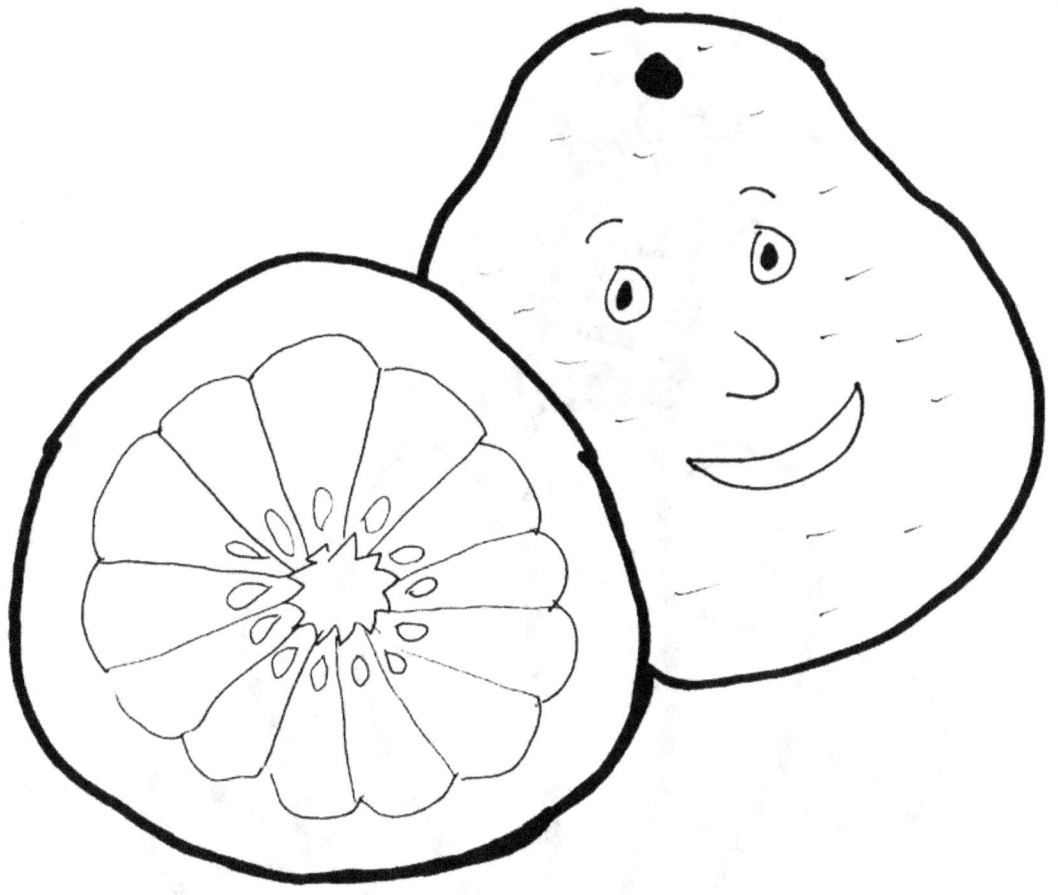

U is for Ugli Fruit

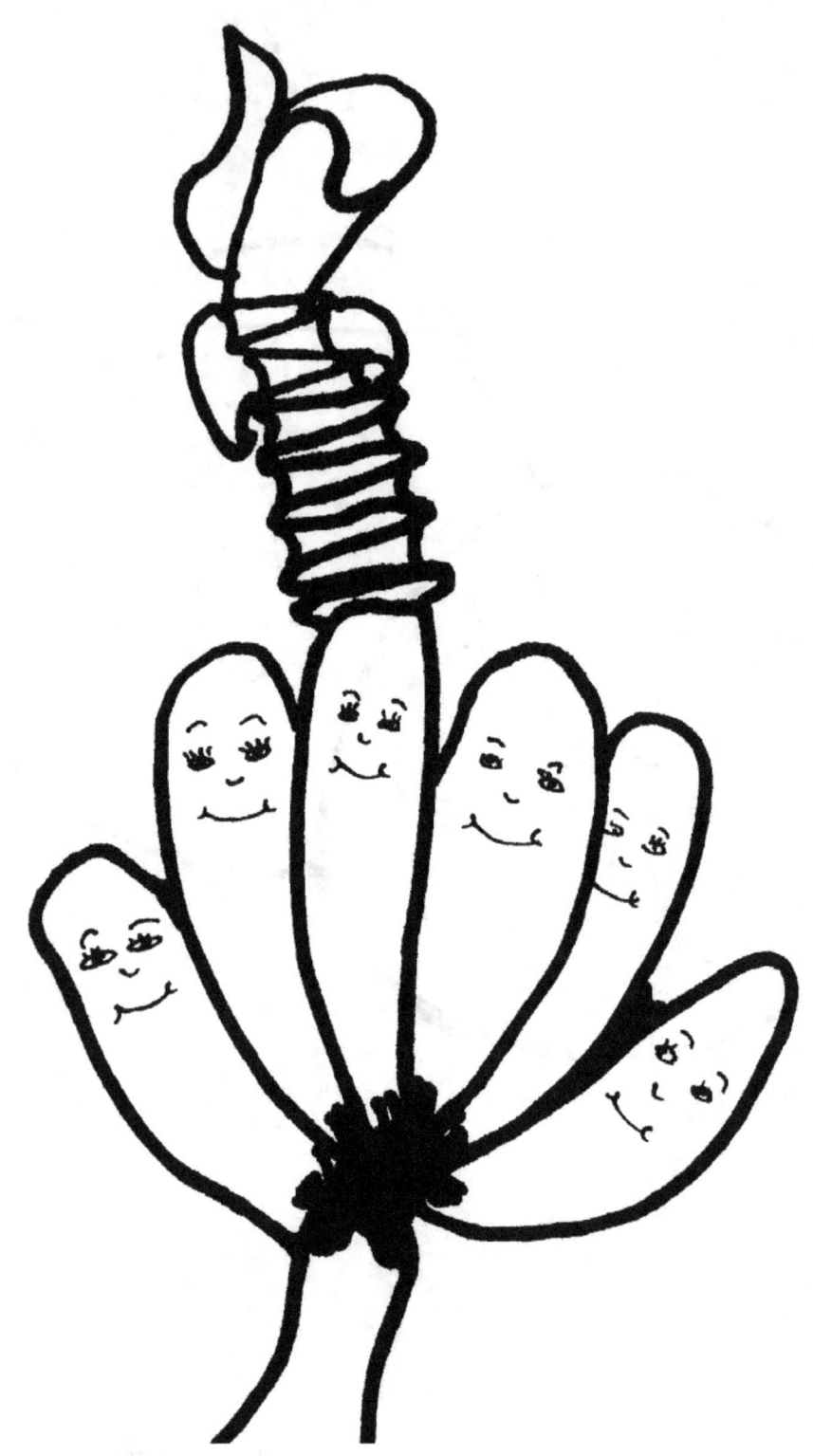

V is for Velvet Pink Bananas

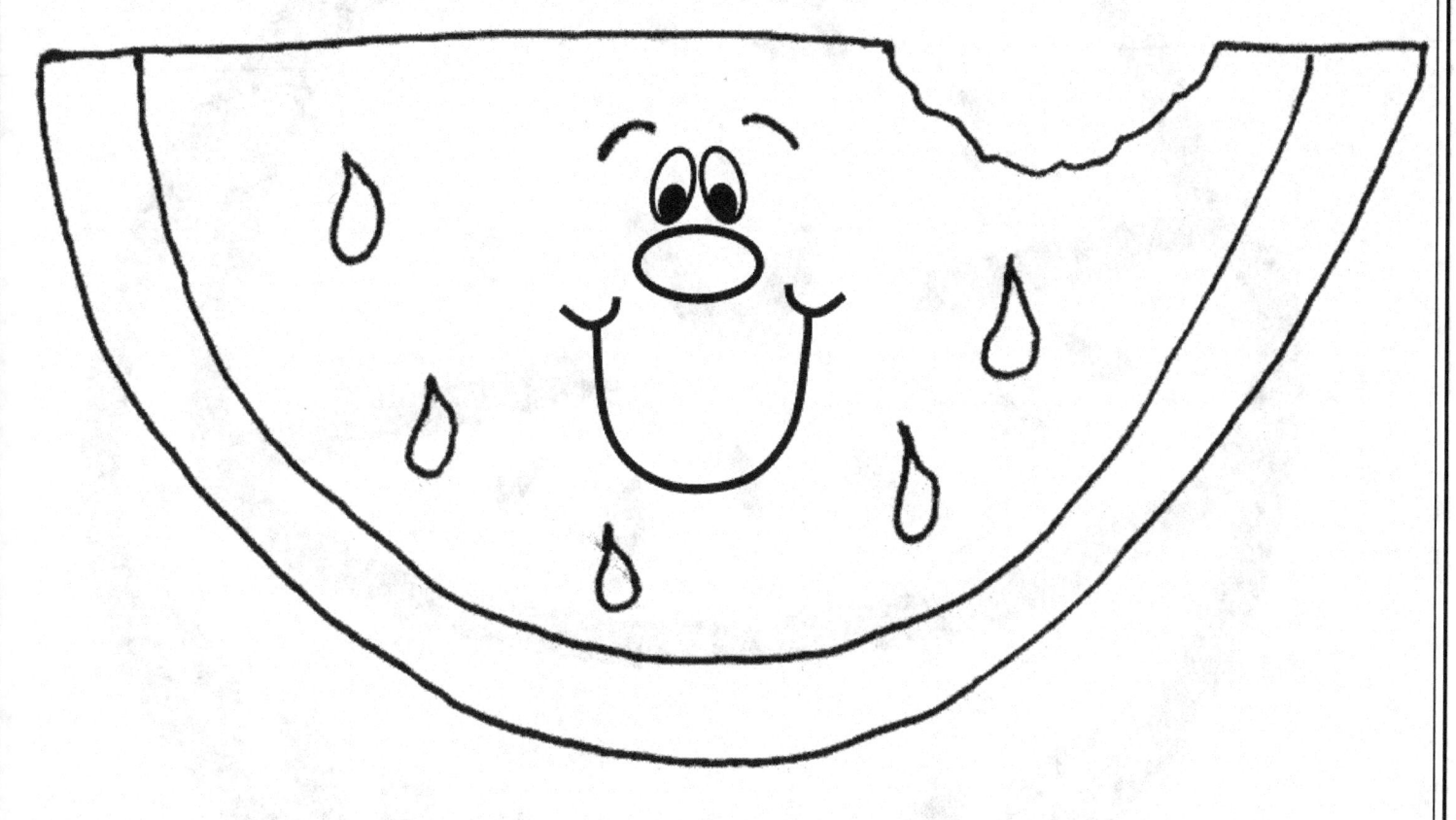

W is for Watermelon

X is for Xigua Melon

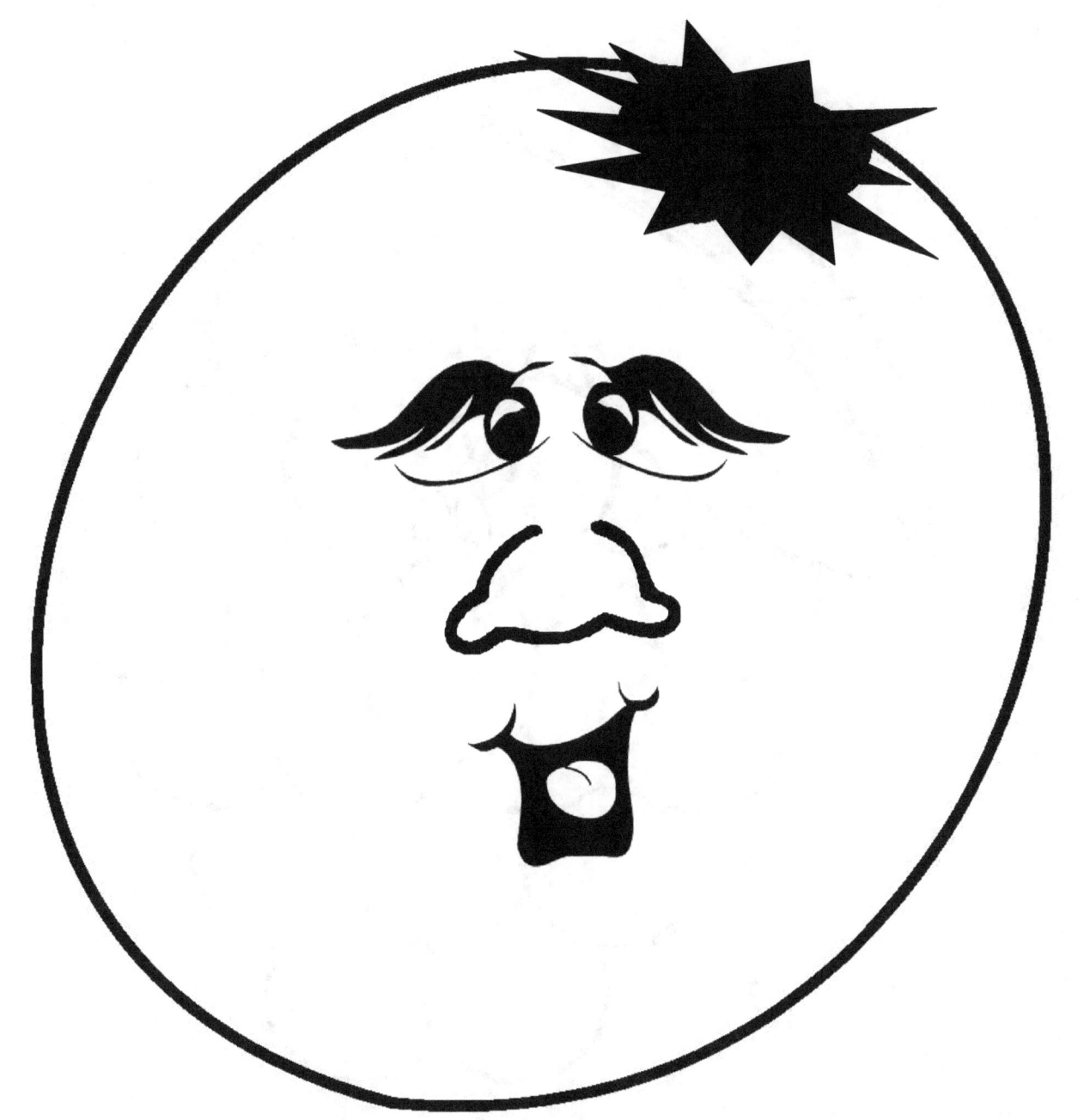

Y is for Yellow Passion Fruit

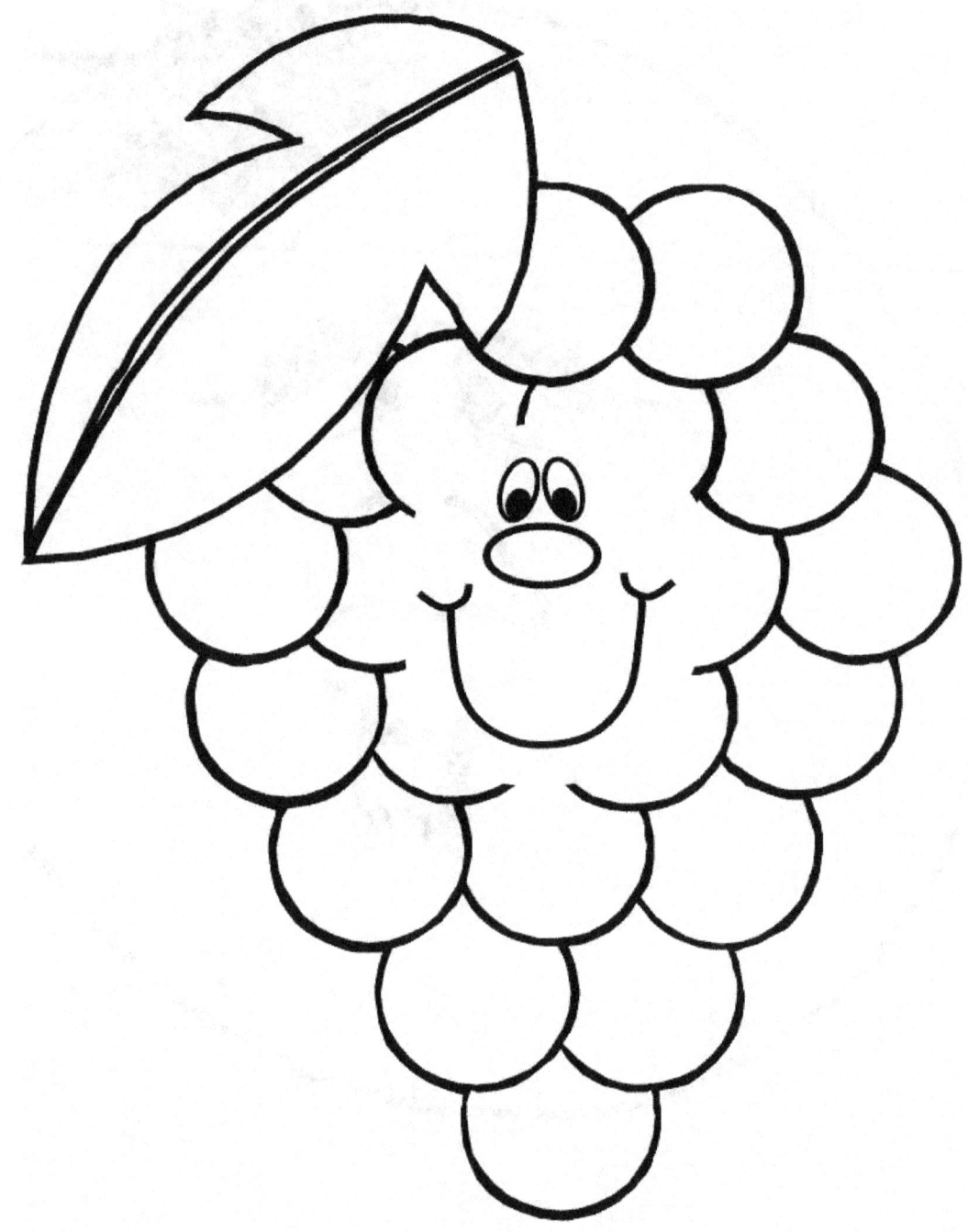

Z is for Zinfandel Grapes

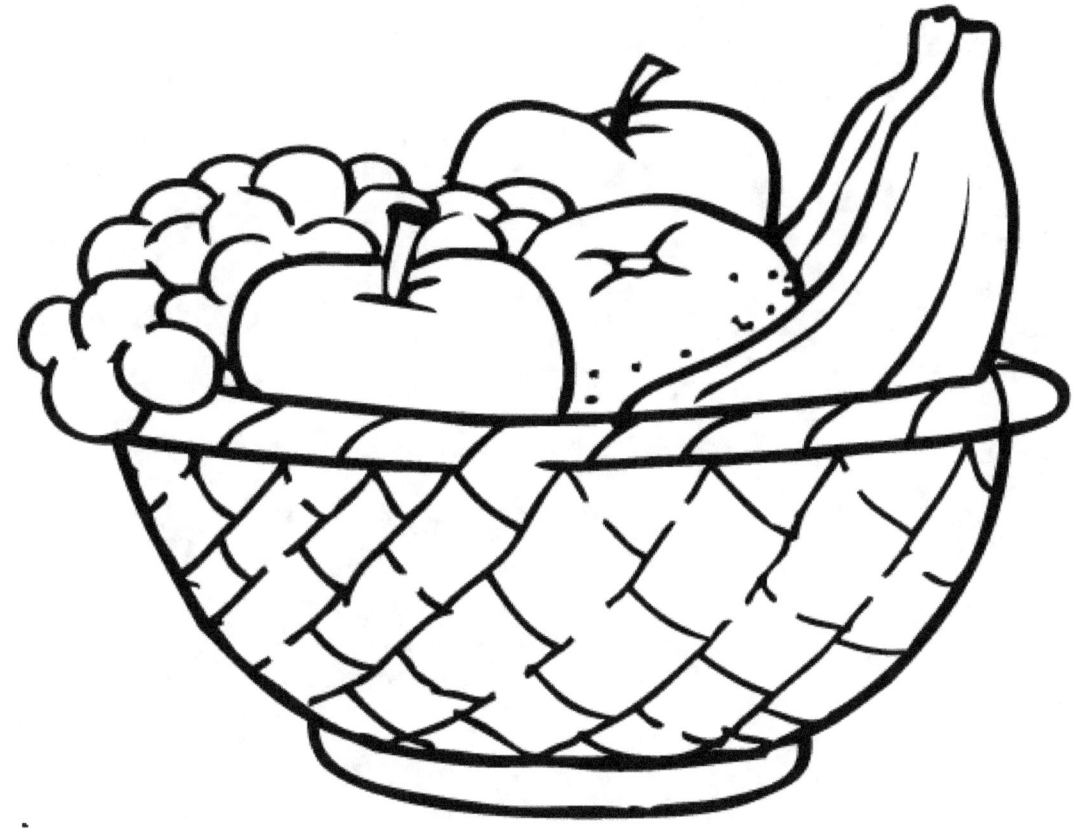

www.ingramcontent.com/pod-product-compliance
Lightning Source LLC
Chambersburg PA
CBHW080448220526
45465CB00007B/2805